To Debz   29ᵗ² July 2014

On the occasion of your
        ordination.

With love & blessings,
        Janet x

MARGARET SILF

LANDSCAPES OF
Prayer

For Gerry and Brian, cherished soul-friends,
guides, and fellow travellers

ONTENTS

THE POWER OF *Landscape*

Our photo albums bulge with memories of landscapes we have loved. Just to browse these memories evokes whole stories about ourselves and our lives and our world.

Of course we can engage with landscape superficially, just by pulling over into the parking area, viewing the distant scene and then moving on, almost untouched by what we have encountered. Or we can become part of a landscape and allow it to become part of us. We can let it penetrate us with something of its spirit, and from then on we will carry that spirit with us wherever we go, however far we may become separated from the beloved land. This happens, for example, when we have inhabited or frequented certain places for a long time, and they have taken root in our souls and left an indelible imprint there. We may discover, perhaps when we have to leave them, that we love them with a power we cannot put into words.

Prayer has its own kind of landscapes, and in our spiritual life too we may engage merely superficially with the mystery that holds us in being, or

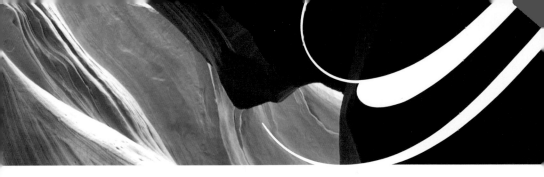

we may go deeper until we feel we are inhabiting the mystery, as we might inhabit a much-loved land, and the mystery is inhabiting us. The deeper we venture, the more powerfully the mystery we call God will shape us and mould us, and we may discover that we love and long to relate to the mystery in ways that ultimately only silence can express.

This book invites you to wander at will through some of the landscapes of your soul, noticing those that touch your heart in a special way at any particular time, and lingering there for as long as you will, to explore what that soul-space means for you. Different spiritual landscapes will speak to you at different times of your life and in different situations. So take time, wherever you find yourself, to be fully present to that space in your heart, so that you might hear more clearly the message that it holds for you.

And as you wander and linger, may you discover ever-deeper layers of the story God is weaving in your life and in our world.

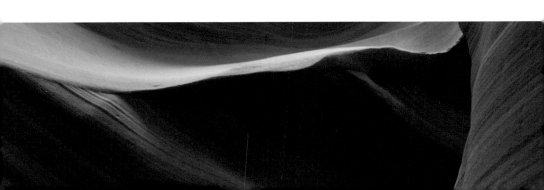

"*The best fertilizer is the gardener's shadow.*"

Author unknown

GARDEN

What, I wonder, does a garden mean for you? Summer days enjoying the scent of new-mown grass and the fragrance of the flowers? Birdsong? Vegetables and herbs that travel only the distance between your kitchen garden and your table? Or maybe hard work, an aching back, an invincible army of weeds?

Would it surprise you to discover that God is in all of these aspects of your heart's garden, and that prayer is to be found in the labour as well as in the love, in the heart's aching as well as in the heart's desire?

The word "paradise", in its ancient Persian, Hebrew, and Greek forms, originally meant "a sacred enclosure". It's easy to see how this idea became the "walled garden" – an evocative image of what prayer can be. I have memories of many beautiful walled gardens, often at the heart of deeply prayerful retreat houses or ancient castles or monasteries, but for today let me introduce you to the smallest ever "walled garden". The story goes that once there was a kindly noble lady who lived in a magnificent mansion. She often used to entertain guests, and one day, as she and a friend were taking tea together, the teapot slipped out of her hand as she was serving her guest. The fine china teapot fell to the ground and its spout and handle broke off. Most people would have thrown it out, I guess, but she loved the teapot, and she gave it a new form of life instead. She made it into a tiny garden. She planted delicate flowers in it, and in time it became its own miniature "sacred enclosure". It reminded her and her guests, every day, that in our brokenness we can be even more lovingly tended and cherished than when we were whole.

Your heart is a garden, the place you go to meet God in prayer, and the place where God meets you, to help you tend the sacredness you share. There will be weeds there, for sure, and maybe brambles and thorns. No human heart is without these. Sometimes, perhaps, it will be good to uproot them, so that they don't spread

any further. And at other times it may be good to leave them and remember that sometimes a "weed" is just a flower we didn't plant, which refuses to submit to our control. There will be desires and yearnings in our garden, striving for the light, like enormous sunflowers, or insinuating themselves into our dreams, like rambling roses. There will be blossoms of pure joy, and other plants that may harbour thorns, stings, or poisonous intentions, like nettles and nightshade.

You will have to work at your garden, if it is to remain a sacred space. Paradise has to be tended. You will need to cultivate your heart's prayer, by watering it regularly with your focused attention, pruning back anything that is growing out of control, turning over the soil as you reflect on your own life and relationships. But you will have help. The birds will serenade you as you toil and will eat the pests that threaten your plants. The bees will pollinate your flowers for you and the worms will ventilate your soil. They all remind us that the garden does not belong to us, but we belong to the garden. We are not in sole charge of anything, not even of ourselves, but we are living cells in the body of all creation, living in mutual inter-dependency with all inhabitants of planet Earth.

A good garden gives life to many creatures as well as to its gardener. In what ways does your heart, your life, give life and nourishment to others? What herbs, such as sincerity or gentleness, grow in your heart and add their special flavour to the feast of life? Does anything you find there threaten to spoil the feast for others? Sarcastic tongues, for example, or spiteful gestures? What gifts bear fruit in your life and bring joy to others? Is there anything in the way you relate to others that threatens to overwhelm them with impatience or intolerance and choke the channels of love? And a garden is a place of loving companionship. Who shares the sacred space of your heart's garden? How lovingly do you share the space of others when they invite you to enter their holy ground?

A MEETING WITH THE GARDENER

In a story from long ago, a grieving woman makes her way at dawn to the garden where she knows her beloved lies in his grave. Tears dim her vision, but even in the dawn light she can see that his body is gone. She cries out in her distress, to the heavens, to the angels, and to a man she suddenly encounters there on the path. She plies him with her questions: Have you seen him? Where have they taken him? He answers with a single word: he calls her name, "Mary!" At that moment she knows she has rediscovered her lost love, in a totally new way. "I took you for the gardener," she falters. "Perhaps I *am* the gardener," he smiles, as they walk away together into the future.

(Adapted from John 20:11–17)

A TIME FOR TENDING

Take a little while in a quiet space to walk around your heart's garden with "the Gardener" and share with him something of how you are feeling. Don't be afraid to show him your truth. He knows it, and loves you anyway.

- How is the weather in your garden this morning? Does your heart feel warm or cold? Is it sunny or foggy, bright or overcast in the core of your being today?

- What season is it? Do you feel alive and full of energy, or heavy in the grip of winter? Is new life burgeoning in you, or are things dying away? What is making you feel more alive? What is tending to deaden you?

- What blossoms do you want to show him, grown from the seeds of love he has planted in your heart? What fruits or gifts from your life would you want to offer him, to share with others?

- Are there any weeds you would like him to deal with?

- Does anything need pruning, and can you ask him for the courage to let him do what needs to be done?

- Are you content to let him be the Gardener, or are you trying to do it all yourself?

Try describing the garden of your heart, either in words or images, to the Gardener in the silence you share, and perhaps also to a trusted friend.

MOUNTAIN

"Do not go where the path may lead; go instead where there is no path and leave a trail."

Ralph Waldo Emerson

I smiled as the bus driver pointed out a local landmark to us. We were driving into the outback, inland from Brisbane, heading for the rainforests of the Lamington National Park. We passed a small hillock, rising up from the flat Queensland plains. The driver, with typical Aussie irony, commented that his Dutch guests always admired this "mountain", never having seen such elevations in their homeland, while the Swiss visitors passed this "molehill" by with barely a second glance. Whatever the Dutch and the Swiss might have thought, however, we would soon be in the mountains of the Great Dividing Range that separates coastal Queensland from the wild uncharted interior. We would be living among the craggy heights, with pademelons, wallabies, exotic birds, and snakes for neighbours. Our climb through the foothills was taking us to landscapes that would open up very different visions from anything we could have seen from the plain.

The Queensland peaks bake in fierce sub-tropical heat. There are others that freeze perpetually in sub-zero Alpine temperatures. I remember a day's ski-ing in Austria that took me to 3,000 metres on pristine snow and under benign blue skies. And then, without warning, the clouds came down and I was lost in the worst swirling whiteout I have ever experienced. Lost, blinded, dizzy, disoriented, and very frightened.

This is another face of the mountain. The mountain will never let us predict its moods. If we seek to scale the mountains of the soul, we should tread lightly and humbly, knowing that we are merely mortal travellers upon the flanks of eternity.

Perhaps this landscape speaks to your place of prayer right now? Perhaps you are yearning to scale heights you have never known before, searching for the fleeting and elusive "peak experience" you may once have known and long to rediscover, when the presence of God was almost palpable? Or perhaps the mountainside has turned to terror as the clouds come down or as the thunder crashes?

Why do we climb mountains? The classic answer is "Because they are there", and this may well be the reason why we long to soar closer to the rarefied peaks of prayer that, we think, only the saints have known. But there are other, more manageable reasons. We climb a mountain to glimpse the view from the top. We climb a mountain to gain a different perspective on our lives and our world. In short, climbing mountains leads us to new vision.

For as long as humankind has been engaged in spiritual searching, we have turned to the mountains for inspiration and challenge, and seen the ascent as a metaphor for our spiritual journey. The climb demands strenuous effort and we may feel daunted at the thought of it. Perhaps it begins fairly gently, as we progress through the foothills, but then the path peters out into mystery. Prayer can be like that. We think we know the form. We use time-honoured techniques to take us deeper into our hearts in search of an encounter with the living God. And the further we think we are going, the more deeply we become lost in the mystery. This can cause us to stand still, alone on the mountainside beneath the endless skies, gazing in wonder at all that the silence reveals. Or it can take us to the centre of our own heart's storms, exposed to elements of ourselves that we had never guessed were there. We reach for the skies, and stumble on the rockfalls. We cherish the solitude of the mountain and yet long for communion and companionship.

The mountain can be a place of transfiguration, where our hearts soar with the eagles and the rocks are bathed in sunlight. Yet there are predators among those very rocks – temptations hitherto unrecognized, demons that can make us or break us. The sun beats down, but tiny flowers are discovered in hidden crevices, shaded by a hand not their own, startling us with their delicate, vulnerable beauty.

Jesus walked both kinds of mountain: the mountain of temptation and the mountain of transfiguration. On the first he faced the worst that the lonely heights could throw at him: heat, hunger, exhaustion, and a confrontation with the secret temptations of his own heart. On the second he not only glimpsed, but became one with, the glory of God transforming a moment in time into the blinding light of the eternal present moment...

TRANSFIGURED

It was early morning as four men began the climb up the mountain. The climb was long and hard. At the top they were glad to rest, and three of them lay down, drowsy and exhausted. The fourth, the one they were following, went aside, apparently in prayer. They watched him, through eyes heavy with sleep, and as they gazed, he seemed to become alive with an inner light that suffused his whole being with brilliance. And beside him stood Moses and Elijah, and the three were deep in conversation. It was a moment in which timelessness broke through all the barriers of human understanding, and cut straight across the ordinary linear narrative of history. The three observers knew they were in sacred space. They wanted to capture the moment, pin it down, erect a shrine. But then, as suddenly as it had come, the moment faded. They were, once more, just four travellers, coming down the mountain, and yet they would never again be the same men who had started the climb early that morning. They had glimpsed a vision of eternity, and such a glimpse will change you for ever.

(Adapted from Luke 9:28–36)

A TIME FOR ENVISIONING

Perhaps there are mountains in your own journey with God? How do you feel about them? What do they mean to you?

- Do you know the "mountain of temptation"? Have you ever felt you were facing your own inner "demons"? How did this experience invite you to grow and discover new strengths in your own weakness?

- Recall any "peak experiences" you have known, when you felt unexpectedly very close to the mystery of God. What seeds did these moments sow in your heart, and what fruits do you feel they may be bearing in your life?

- Peak experiences such as these connect us more intimately with God without separating us from the earth. How have you "earthed" your mountain experiences, bringing the treasure of that rare intimacy down to the valley of your everyday life?

- What new perspectives about the wider world around you and the secret world within you has the mountain peak offered you?

- What is the nature of the special vision that is trying to come to birth in *your* life? Dare you follow your dreams?

We journey for many miles and climb many winding rocky paths before we glimpse the vision from the peak, and almost before we can grasp it, it is gone, so fleeting are our moments of light. Remember yours in gratitude and cherish them in your heart. You did not find them. *They* found *you*, and they are making a difference in ways you cannot guess.

SEASHORE

"I hear the slow ticktock of the planet when I stand in a salt marsh or walk the sands of Miramar."

Richard Bode, *Beachcombing at Miramar*

There's no telling what you might find along the seashore. My own family, on my mother's side, hail from the north-east of Scotland. During a visit with an aunt and uncle up in Peterhead one time, I sat for a while on a rocky outcrop, watching the sea, and thinking of the many times Jesus too walked the shoreline, talking with friends, telling stories, making breakfast even…. Overhead the screaming seagulls registered their protest at my presence. Down at the harbour the fishermen were preparing their nets, talking in the broad Buchanie dialect of that part of Scotland, and I wondered how they would have reacted to an invitation from a stranger to follow him into an unknown and uncertain future. Suddenly the air was pierced by a sharp cry of delight from my aunt. She had spotted a piece of old fishing net on the beach, and thought it might make a good garden ornament. We investigated and found it to be a very large, abandoned net of which only the rim remained, the middle having been completely torn away – perhaps by some extraordinarily large catch. Then, as we were sitting on the old net, gazing out to sea, the next surprise arrived – the distinct scent of a barbecue drifting across the cliff-side. We later discovered a caravan site just over the hill, but for those few moments I was back in Galilee, and a stranger on the shore was beckoning us to join him for a fish breakfast.

The seashore is a moving boundary between the predictability of dry land and the restless mystery of the ocean. To walk the seashore is to allow the mystery to touch the edges of our everyday world. Sometimes that touch is the gentle lapping of waves that have spent all their force out at sea. Sometimes it is the terrifying crash of breakers that have saved up all their energy, it seems, to bombard our quiet lives. Sometimes a baby can paddle in it. Sometimes its power can destroy our homes and our lives.

When I walk the seashore, I meet, in that one sacred space, both the immanent and the transcendent God. The ocean stretches out as far as my eye can see, and way beyond, just as the sense of the divine lies far beyond any human understanding. And yet that same ocean laps at my feet and deposits all kinds of very ordinary objects on the shore for me to discover as I do my beachcombing – objects that may have stories to tell me about who I am and who God is for me, and how our realities embrace in this ordinary–extraordinary space where the water meets the land.

I look out to sea, and get a glimpse of the secret life of the ocean, its hidden beauty and its hidden fears, and they speak to my heart of my own hidden possibilities and unspoken fears. I see, in the ocean, the cradle of all life on earth, and I want to thank the universe for this miracle, that we exist at all, and to recommit myself to living in a way that is worthy of the divine intention and desire that keeps on dreaming us into being.

I watch the boats putting out for another day's fishing. They are so fragile, so vulnerable, and yet they follow, every day, that invitation to "put out into deeper water and let down your nets for a catch". Life calls me into deeper water too, in the challenges that lie ahead, at work, in the family, in the world. My own little vessel is fragile and vulnerable. Anything could happen out there. I feel out of my depth in so much of what is happening in my life. And yet that call echoes within me too: trust the deeper water; come; follow!

BREAKFAST ON THE SHORE

It had been a terrible night. The devastation, despair, and disillusionment that came in the wake of the execution of their friend had robbed them of any desire to do anything, ever again. So they went back to the one thing they thought they knew how to do. They went fishing. But even the fish were absent from that night that was full of absence in every way. The new day crept slowly, reluctantly, grey and listless, across the water.

They heard the voice before they saw the man. "Caught anything, lads?" it enquired. "You *are* joking!" came their answer. That might have been it. Just an early greeting from an unseen stranger on the shore. But the voice went on, insistently, pushing through the pre-dawn gloom: "Put down the nets on the other side of the boat, and see what happens." Their response to this unsolicited advice remains unrecorded! But they did as the voice suggested. And, for sure, the catch almost broke the net!

Then they saw him, as the sunrise cast its glow over his eager face. "Come on shore and have some breakfast," he invited them. The smell of the barbecue wafted across the waves to them, and it was way sweeter than the scent of any incense could ever be. It beckoned them to the shore, to breakfast, and a new beginning.

(Adapted from John 21:1–14)

TIME FOR BEACHCOMBING

Beachcombing is a wonderful way to pray. You might like to try it. You don't need a beach or an ocean to do it. Just a little time, a little patience, open eyes and an open heart.

"Beachcombing" is another way of describing the ancient form of prayer variously known as the "Review of the Day" or the *Examen*. The "beach" is simply the experience of your day, just as it was, with all its ups and downs, its beautiful shells and its stinging jellyfish. To make this kind of prayer, just wander along that "beach" and see what you find. Your morning (or evening or anytime) prayer-stroll might look a bit like this:

- What has happened today to delight you, to give you a glimpse of joy, to make you feel more alive, more connected to God, to yourself or to others?

- Who or what has nourished you in some way today, or helped to heal a hurt?

- Has the surf of your own life, the things you have said and done today, brought nourishment, healing, or a loving touch to someone else's beach?

- Has anything happened today, or been said or done, that has triggered feelings of anger or sorrow or resentment in you? What do you think was at the root of those feelings?

- As you look back over your beach today, notice the trail of your footprints. Is there anything you regret in the path you have walked today, or anything you would want to handle differently tomorrow? If so, simply let it rest there between you and God, without judging yourself or anyone else.

As you bring your prayer to a close, gather up the treasures of your beachcombing, store them away in your heart, and then let the incoming tide wash everything else away. Tomorrow you will walk once more on virgin sand.

"*Between every two pines is a doorway to a new world.*"

John Muir

FOREST

Once upon a time a little girl lived in a house in the middle of a very dense, dark forest. Because the forest held many dangers, her parents had always warned her never to go out alone, but one day, temptation became too great to resist, and she ventured out alone. Thrilled at her new-found freedom she set off gleefully, without paying attention to where she was going, and very soon she was completely lost. Frightened and alone she searched desperately for the way home. As night began to fall her father came out to look for the lost child. He walked through the forest, frantic with anxiety. The stars and the moon came out, but there was still no sign of her. At last, when half the dark night had passed, he found her, huddled at the foot of a tall tree, covered with leaves, fast asleep.

And what do you imagine the frantic father said when he found his disobedient daughter? Well, when she awoke and realized what had happened, she was sure that he would punish her for going off into the forest alone. Instead, he picked her up and carried her home in his arms. "We will talk about this tomorrow," he promised as he tucked her up into her own little bed. The next morning he sat down with the child on his lap. She expected him to be angry, but all he did was take out a bag of shiny white pebbles from his pocket. "These are for you," he said. "You are growing up now and I know that there will be times when you will have to

walk through the forest alone. You will be confused, and sometimes lost. Remember always to take these pebbles with you, and from the moment you leave your home, be sure to drop a pebble every few yards as you walk. If you do this, then wherever you stray, you will always be able to follow the trail of pebbles and they will lead you back home."

Perhaps you often feel, too, that you are lost, going round in circles, unable to see the wood for the trees? Perhaps you feel fearful and alone, and you can see no obvious pattern either in your prayer or in your life? Perhaps the forest is dark and there are no waymarks, and you can't see any clear paths ahead? If we are honest, we all know something of those enchanted forests in our own lives, with their doubts, confusions, darkness, fears, and aloneness. Perhaps you feel you have lost touch with the centre of your being, lost the habit of spending time in the stillness of your soul, lost your way with God? If your prayer feels at all like this, you might like to pause a while in the forest.

Yet forests are magical places in a very real way. Remember your own favourite forest. I think mine would be Muir Woods (named after the Scottish naturalist John Muir) near San Francisco, where the giant sequoias soar to the skies and form a vast natural cathedral, where even the noisiest visitor treads softly and speaks quietly, in reverence for the natural holiness

in that place. Let's follow the invitation of these majestic trees, simply to stand still and allow earth and heaven to meet within us. Let's listen to the whispers of wisdom from these gentle, silent giants.

Trees put down deep roots, seeking nourishment, water and a place of belonging. Our being too has deep roots, sustaining us through all that life throws at us. The space of prayer we might call the forest invites us to become still and quiet and to reconnect with those deep roots. What nourishes your heart? What ground water feeds the depths of your soul? Where is your place of belonging? Where, and with whom, do you feel rooted and grounded?

Trees raise their crowns to the heavens, straining towards the sun, the source of their natural energy. They spread their branches out to embrace the world around them, and to give shelter to the birds and other creatures of the forest – the squirrels, the chipmunks, the possums. Their leaves give us oxygen, their blossoms give us joy, their fruits give us food. Which parts of your life give life to the world? Which aspects of your heart most long to reach out to others? What fruits does your life give to those around you? Simply stand still in your inner forest, and let these questions rise to consciousness. Simply notice your own roots and your own crown, your own unique and necessary place in the forest.

Sometimes, when we feel hopelessly lost, we will find ourselves again simply by standing still. The answer to our unspoken question "Wherever am I?" lies right there in our own hearts. "You are who you are, and you rest in my peace. Be still and know this truth." We don't have to retrace our steps to anywhere. We simply have to be still, and become aware once more, at the deepest level of our souls, of the reality that holds us in being. The "shiny white pebbles" of our own experience, those memories of times when God has felt close by and we knew where we belonged, can guide us to that still centre, as surely as they might guide a lost traveller back home.

If we can do this, then any threats we felt the forest held for us can dissolve into precious gifts: shelter from the storm and shade from the fierce sunlight; luxuriant growth where we perhaps thought we were barren; ancient wisdom deep at the tips of our roots, where we least expected it. And if we think we are utterly insignificant in the scheme of things, a mere acorn on the forest floor, let us remind ourselves that in the smallest acorn lies a mighty forest, waiting only for time to bring it to birth.

PLANTED BY THE STREAM

It is a wise and blessed soul that doesn't waste itself running after the whims of the moment and joining in the gossip of the market-place. Such a soul is like a tree planted beside living water, putting down deep roots to where its true nourishment is found. The heat cannot destroy it, nor the dry season cause it to wither. On the contrary, because it is connected to the source of its being, its leaves will not fall, nor shall it cease to bear fruit. Take this tree's wisdom as your model, and remain rooted and planted in the heart of the source of all life, returning to that deep root whenever the storms shake you and the paths confuse.

(Adapted from Jeremiah 17:5–8 and Psalm 1)

A TIME FOR SEARCHING

Every life gets lost in the forest from time to time. If you feel you are in such a place at present, listen to the wisdom of the trees. The answer to your searching may be hidden right there in the very place where you feel yourself to be so lost. It is hidden deep within the tree that you can't see for the forest. Let your heart come to stillness and reflect:

- How deep are your roots and what really nourishes your soul?

- Is anything distracting or preoccupying you, and causing you to run round in circles after things that really don't matter?

- Outwardly it may be autumn, and you feel like a stripped tree, but if your roots go deep, there is a springtime gestating inside every winter. Can you trust this?

- What "memory pebbles" of your own experience have the power to lead you back to the place where your heart is at home?

- Your life, like a tree, is an indispensable part of a mighty forest. What fruits would you want it to bear for all the creatures of that forest?

Take a moment to recall a forest you have loved, and walk its pathways in your imagination. Let its timeless stillness bring you peace, clarity, and new directions.

RIVER

"*Even Stalin could not stop the river from entering people's dreams again, the river with its long memory and the eternal present.*"

Anne Michaels, *The Winter Vault*

You can keep on going to the same river, and even the same spot on the riverbank, but you will never see the same water twice. Rivers are wonderful teachers of how the continuum of our being can be perfectly balanced with the immediate present moment. The river reveals an endless cycle of life, flowing from an almost imperceptible source, through all the shifting scenes of our lives, continually striving towards its destiny in the ocean, there to be taken up again as cloud, and to fall once more on the high ground, to become another river. And all the while it brings life. Above all else the river is the bringer of life. There is growth where there is water.

Water is more powerful than stone; it can literally move mountains, simply by a slow and steady flow or even a slow and steady drip. And yet it does not flaunt its strength. Instead, it yields to the lie of the land, and the pull of gravity, and the presence of obstacles in its way. It doesn't stop to cry about what blocks it, but it finds a way round the obstacle, and in doing so it waters a larger area of land than it could otherwise have done. It never tries to hold on to the moment, but flows with it, letting go, moment after moment – letting go, in order to embrace what lies ahead. Letting go, letting flow.

A story tells how a stream flowed through hills and dales, and eventually came to the edge of a desert. It pitched itself in vain at the desert sand, but every time it did so it simply drained away into nothing. At last the wind intervened, and shared its wisdom with the stream. "If you want to cross the desert," it whispered to the stream, "you have to surrender yourself to the wind and be taken up into the cloud, and then let yourself be carried across the desert." The stream protested at first, at this apparent loss of identity, but eventually surrendered, and the cloud and the wind carried its essence across the desert, where it fell again in a new place, a new stream, a new source of life.

What does the image of the river mean to you? You might look at the course of your own life in terms of the flow of a river. Where was its source and what or who were its early tributaries – those people, family or strangers, contemporary or long-dead, who influenced your way of seeing things? How has the river flowed, through the years of your life? For most of us there will have been times of quiet flow, but also "white water" times when our lives hit the rapids. Sometimes the flow will have been brisk and clear and healthy, and at other times your life may have felt stagnant and sluggish, or even polluted. Perhaps the power of your river will have

generated energy and inspiration for others, and perhaps sometimes you may feel your own energy has been hijacked to serve the purposes of other people, or siphoned off to be stored and shared among many? Through what kinds of landscape has your river flowed? You may recall wilderness times, and times of great fruitfulness. Remember that your river may have brought life to others' deserts, and nourished the dreams and aspirations of many, perhaps unknown to you. So where is your river now, and how is its flow? How do you feel about its meanderings so far, and what are your hopes and dreams for its future course?

An ancient mystic tells a story about a river that could offer us a picture of our spiritual journey. This is how he describes his vision…

A RIVER OF LIFE

My guide showed me a stream that had its origin in the sanctuary, but flowed out from there, under the threshold, all round the outside of the building, and finally found its course in the wider world. A man was trying to measure the river. Using a measuring rod he calculated a certain distance of the river's flow, and asked me to wade across the stream at this point. I did so and the water came up to my ankles. He measured a further span downstream, and asked me to cross again. Now the water came up to my knees. A third time he measured off a span of the river, even further downstream, and at this point the water reached my waist. When he made his final measurement, and asked me to wade across again, it was impossible. By this point the river had become so deep and fast-flowing that I couldn't have crossed it. I was out of my depth.

Only when I realized that I couldn't measure the flow of the river of life, and nor could he, did I see the river from a different perspective. Now it was no longer about how we could measure it out or cross it. Now the focus was entirely upon the river itself. I saw what the river was really about. I saw the fish swimming in it, healthy and full of life, and fishermen on the riverbanks. I noticed that the marshes and salty lagoons along the course of the river came to fresh life when the living stream flowed through them, but that where this flow was blocked or denied or resisted, they remained lifeless and stagnant. I saw that the riverbanks were lined with many different trees, each bearing fruit in its season, and with leaves that provided medicinal cures. And all this life, I came to understand, was sustained because the flow of the river of life had its source in the very heart of God, the Life-giver.

(Adapted from Ezekiel 47:1–12)

TIME FOR LETTING GO AND LETTING FLOW

The subject of the story learns that although he can appear to have things "measured up" and under control, in fact the river flows its own course, and is its own reality. Only after this insight has been arrived at can we see the river of life for what it really is, the source of life for all creation, and not something we can ever package up for our own purposes. And the *raison d'être* of the river is always to strive for the greatest possible fullness of life for all creation. Only when this is our desire too will we find ourselves swimming in harmony with the deep currents of life and of God.

- Prayer can flow like a river, following a sometimes winding course reflecting the terrain of our everyday lives, not subject to all our plans and programmes, but finding its own natural direction. Do you feel comfortable letting your prayer flow in this way, not knowing perhaps at any given time exactly "how" you are praying?

- Reflecting on the course of your life in terms of a river is a prayer in itself. Try drawing or describing in words, to yourself or to a trusted friend, how your river has flowed and is continuing to flow.

- In what ways is your river bringing life to the world beyond yourself? In what ways are the rivers of others' lives nourishing *you*?

- Can you risk being "out of your depth", and letting your focus shift from yourself and how you are doing, to the river and the life it is bringing, recognizing yourself as a part of that flow of life?

- The river never stands still. It has to continually let go of yesterday in order to bring life to tomorrow. Is there anything you need to let go of, in order that you might be free to keep on becoming the person God is dreaming you to be?

A river is always part of a greater cycle, and our prayer, too, is always part of a greater conversation, a single note in a great symphony. The river remembers your story and all our stories and carries their treasure with it to its destiny in the ocean of God's love. And even as it flows it calls us to be where we are, and who we are, in the only moment we have, the eternal present moment.

"When I added the dimension of time to the landscape of the world, I saw how freedom grew the beauties and horrors from the same live branch."

Annie Dillard, *Pilgrim at Tinker Creek*

JUNGLE

The dominant colour is green, green, and more green. Every shade of green. The colour of luxuriant growth and God's over-the-top fecundity. And then a new presence darts across the scene – a magnificent butterfly, threading a trail of vibrant colour through the weaving of the sea of green. As I gaze through the soaring bamboos to the distant hills of the Malaysian heartlands, this butterfly speaks to me of both the splendour and the struggle of the jungle and reminds me of the story of the little boy in the school science laboratory, who was eagerly watching the emergence of a butterfly from its cocoon. As the butterfly began its struggle to get free

of the tangled threads that held it, the boy took pity on it, and tried to shorten its battle into life by cutting through the threads that seemed to be imprisoning it. The butterfly died. The birth struggle had been essential, to pump the necessary strength into its wings to enable it to fly. Without struggle there is no life. The wrestling is part of the revealing. It is in our striving that we grow, just as these soaring bamboos live out their lives between searing heat, torrential rain, and almost daily tropical storms as they reach for the tropical skies above them.

Most of us don't live in the jungle, and may never enter such a space physically. Yet the jungle is all around us. The human jungle. The urban jungle. These are the places where *we* live out our lives, and they are not called "jungles" for nothing. The jungle is a place of almost overwhelming and fast-moving growth, and home to an incredible diversity of life. Ethnic diversity. Cultural diversity. A wide and often conflicting diversity of opinion. Amazing things are gestating there. Who knows what gifts are latent in those children running wild in our streets? Who can guess what tenderness is in the hearts of the mothers in the ghetto, or what courage in the ones who dare to speak their truth when their principles run up against

the contrary tides of public opinion? Who can tell what new visions are being forged in the heat of our hostilities?

It's hard going, pushing your way forward through the entanglements of a society that seems to be running out of control. So often there is no obvious way forward at all. Sometimes the threatening nature of jungle life terrifies us. We know there are significant dangers lurking in the undergrowth from unseen predators: street crime; addiction; moral ambivalence; domestic violence… the list goes on and on. We live out our days, all too often, in a mindset of wariness, distrust, and fear. We never know when we might tread on a dangerous snake or have our lunch stolen by an over-attentive monkey or its urban equivalent. Such hazards walk our city streets as surely as they inhabit the Malaysian jungles.

Yet the jungle challenges our spirit of adventure too. It invites us to risk the pioneering journey through the obstacles we meet in the long and arduous process of becoming who we truly are. It is no accident that so many archetypal stories tell of how the beautiful princess can only be reached by the prince who has the courage to struggle through the dense and fearsome forests to liberate her. We are both prince and princess in our own stories. There is a pearl of great price to be discovered, but it will only be found if we risk the struggle to penetrate the entanglements of our fears.

What might prayer mean in these circumstances? Can we really stay close to God and our deepest selves amid this jungle warfare we call "life"?

THE MAN WHO WAS ALL OVER THE PLACE

He had always been something of an outcast. Now, everyone agreed, he was out of control and so he was chained up in the cemetery, like one possessed, every so often tearing his chains apart and dragging the tombstones out of the ground and hurling them through the air. He saw the Healer coming, and immediately knew him for who he was. "Leave me alone," he pleaded. "Don't come here to torment me." "Be calm," came a gentle voice in response. "Tell me your name." "Call me legion," the man replied, "because there are a hundred different 'me's. I'm all over the place. Can't you see?" "I tell you, that it is only your fears that are 'legion'" the Healer reassured him. "Let me draw the terrors away from you, and the landscape of your heart will cease to be a jungle full of shadows and threats." Nearby a herd of pigs took fright and bolted off in panic, down towards the lake. Anyone watching might have thought the chained man's fears had transferred themselves to the pigs; he himself became utterly calm. He sat down beside his rescuer. The jungle had lost its terrors, because something much greater had moved in to reveal its essential beauty and integrity.

(Adapted from Luke 8:26–39)

TIME FOR STRUGGLING AND FOR CEASING TO STRUGGLE

While our own experience of contemporary jungles, whether in our cities or in our hearts, will not usually be as dramatic as the struggle described in this story, we can also feel, with the chained man, that we are "all over the place" and that the wild side of our lives and our society is chaining us and threatening us in ways we can hardly articulate. Like him, we know the terrors that stalk us silently, in our dreams and in our streets. But can we also discover the calm that heals him?

If your own life feels like a jungle at present, perhaps your prayer might be exploring questions like these:

- Where do you see the beauty of the life being lived around you, especially in places where it is not beautiful? What brings colour and vibrancy to the sometimes grim shadows of the streets?

- What frightens you most in the world around you? Could compassion, patience, a listening ear, or a more informed understanding do anything to address these fears and their root causes?

- In what ways is your own heart a jungle, where anxieties, fears and obsessions roam unchecked? Does anything within you strike you as being "out of control"? Is there anything you would want to chain up and banish to the subconscious world? How do you think the Healer would speak to those things in your heart?

- Sometimes it feels as if we are wading through treacle just to make one single step. How might you find a pathway through the entanglements of your experience? The Healer restored the "legion" of the deranged man to a new wholeness and oneness. We make our way through the undergrowth of our complicated lives by taking one step at a time. Where do you think your next step should be?

- Where is your sense of adventure? Dare you allow your life to go "out of control" sometimes, in order to break through to new possibilities?

Life, not death, is the final word in the drama of creation. In all our prayer, let the flavour of the sweet fruit, the fragrance of the unexpected flower, the bright plumage of the swooping bird, the courage to take another step, the radical fecundity of all we are and all we can become be the offerings we bring to the altar of our hearts, for these are more powerful than all our fears.

DESERT

"Emptiness offers answers of its own.
Deep speaks to deep."

Belden Lane, ***The Solace of Fierce Landscapes***

Sand is for sifting. In our desert spaces we find ourselves confronting our own emptiness, in which both our angels and our demons may visit us. In the desert we learn discernment, by sifting through our experience, our memories, our desires, discovering which of them lead to life and which to death. The heat of the desert day leaves us nowhere to hide from ourselves, and the cold of the night reminds us that without the constant flow of grace and divine energy we cannot exist. It will test us to the limits, reveal our limitations, uncover our weakness and show up our illusions for what they really are. The desert is a place of extremes that can kill us or bring us unexpected joy; a place that may reveal the worst in us and bring the best to birth.

We are in the Sinai Desert. The climb, which began in the middle of the night, has brought us to the flanks of Mount Sinai. The sun rose two or three hours ago, and now the temperature is becoming hostile. Sharing what water we still have we are making slow and thirsty progress down to the monastery that nestles in its own man-made oasis in the plain. As we make our descent, we come upon a wandering Bedouin who invites us to share some of the aromatic tea he is brewing from the herbs that grow nearby, struggling into brief existence in the sand and the scrub. We accept with joyful gratitude and sit with him in a small circle around his campfire. There could hardly have been more joy had we stumbled upon a burning bush, so welcome is that tea and that unsolicited kindness.

Greatly encouraged and enlivened, and reassured of our place in the human family, and the goodwill of most of our fellow human beings, we arrive at the courtyard of the monastery, where there is a water pump. One of our group, a young boy, barely more than a child, goes up to fill his water bottle there, but he is intercepted and told that he may not take the water. It belongs to the monastery.

If this were a court of law, and I the counsel for the prosecution, I would rest my case now and have little doubt that the jury could be trusted to arrive at the right verdict as to which aspects of that day's experience

came from the angels and which from the demons, which contributed something to the fullness of life and which diminished it.

The process of discernment is a bit like that. We look back over the events of a day, or a week, and reflect on what went on – especially what went on in our own hearts. Where did the angels leave a footprint on our day, perhaps in something someone said or did, or in something we ourselves said or did – something that made the whole of creation a little bit more alive? And where do we notice the hoofprint of the demons: the sarcastic rejoinder that we couldn't resist; the selfish withholding of something that could have helped another person; the not-quite-true piece of gossip that we just had to pass on?

There is a story about a little girl who came to visit her grandmother, bringing a tale about someone else in her class at school. The grandmother stopped her right there at the start of the story. "Before you tell me this story," she said, "first ask yourself whether it will go through three sieves. The first asks: Is it true? The second: Is it kind? The third: Is it necessary?" Good ground rules, learned from a lifetime of sifting.

When we are in a desert space we may find it difficult to put our prayers into words. We experience dryness and emptiness, and we wonder what happened to the experiences of spiritual consolation we remember from other stages of our journey. We may even doubt ourselves and the whole spiritual enterprise, and wish we had never set out. We are not alone in encountering such a space. Most of those who have walked the pathways of prayer before us will have come to this wilderness space where it becomes impossible to impose our human patterns upon the mystery we call God. In the desert we have no option but to let God be God.

There is one imperative that will never fail us…

CHOOSE LIFE!

Ancient wisdom records a "conversation" between God and humankind that took place long ago and yet still holds completely true for us today. It went something like this:

What I am inviting you to discover, and to live by, is not something exotic or remote, nor is it hard to understand. It lies well within your own ability and your own reach. It isn't high up in the sky so that you have to go into outer space to access it, or beyond the horizon, so that however far you travel in search of it you will never reach it. Not at all! In fact it is closer to you than you are to yourself. This deep truth that you really can live by is within you – actually in your own heart. All you need to do is stay in touch with it, and live true to it.

And this is how it is, in the simplest terms. If you live true to the truth at the core of your being – a truth that I, your God, have planted there – call it your conscience, or your inner compass or whatever you will – then you will live in harmony with all creation and at peace within yourself. If you choose to ignore or go against this inner truth, you will be choosing a path that leads not to life in all its fullness, but to death, and you will damage the rest of creation along with yourself. And so today, and every day, I offer you two choices: blessing or curse, healing or harming, life or death. In everything you do and say and think, therefore, choose life!

(Adapted from Deuteronomy 30:15–20)

TIME FOR SIFTING

The call of the desert is simple and clear: choose life! Let go of all lesser considerations, all illusions, and in every situation choose what your heart knows to be the more loving, the more life-giving, the more truly human thing to do next. The prayer of discernment may help you do some sifting...

- Take some time to sift through your immediate and recent experience. What aspects of your life do you feel are life-giving, for yourself and others? Are there any aspects that you feel are diminishing the fullness of life for yourself or others, or for all creation?

- Some relationships help us to grow. Others seem to diminish us. How do you see your own relationships in this light? How do you think others might view the relationships they have with you? If you detect any shadows here, might it be possible to talk with those concerned and perhaps put the relationship on a more life-giving footing, or, if you feel it is necessary, move away from it?

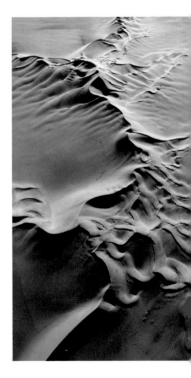

- Traditionally, in the badlands of a desert region, absolutely nothing grows and any human travellers are risking their lives if they venture too far. The badlands may look very enticing, and, like temptations to do what we know to be wrong, seduce us into exploring their challenging crags and gullies. Are there any "badlands" in your heart's landscape?

• In the desert we are especially vulnerable to illusions; for example we may think we see an oasis, and we may go off course to reach it, and when we get there we discover it was just a trick of the light. Take an honest look at some of the things you are aiming at in your life. Could any of them be illusions? Don't be afraid if your illusions get shattered. Illusions are good things to lose. In their absence we can more clearly see the truth about ourselves.

• Every so often, and incredibly beautifully, the desert blooms. What rare gifts have you discovered in times when you felt your heart was dry and parched? Gather such fragile flowers of joy and cherish them forever.

In the desert one must never be without water. In our hearts' deserts that water is the rain of grace. The desert blooms when the rains come. Our hearts bloom when they are soaked by the rains of grace. But between the showers of unexpected and unearned grace, our daily water comes from taking time and space to be consciously in the presence of God. Whatever form that prayer of presence takes for you – formal or informal, in words or in silence, in a special place, or wherever you happen to be – make sure you stay connected to it. It is your water supply in a waterless world. Don't set off, even for a day, without it.

CAVE

"*Even if I should be locked up in a narrow cell and a cloud should drift past my small barred window, then I shall bring you that cloud, O God, while there is still the strength in me to do so.*"

Etty Hillesum: An Interrupted Life – Written just over a year before her death in Auschwitz

Caves have always been a part of my inner landscape. I grew up close to the caverns of the Peak District in the English Pennines, and often visited them as a child, gazing in amazement at the colourful mineral traces, and the stalagmites and stalactites. But it was in South Africa that I encountered two different kinds of cave that truly inspired me.

The first was in a part of the southern Drakensberg Mountains, just south of the little mountain kingdom of Lesotho. We had come down from Lesotho and were staying with a friend at her farmstead. Those days would open my eyes to many things, including the cost our friend had had to pay for her resistance to apartheid. But the cave was a wholly unexpected gift. We reached it after a hair-raising ride over the veld and a steep descent on

foot into a hidden valley. Our guide, who declared himself to be "not religious" paused at the entrance, as if about to enter a cathedral, and we sensed the sacredness of this ancient space. He led us to its innermost recesses, and there we gazed upon hundreds of symbolic figures: animals, hunters, figures half-human half-animal, figures in the process of transformation, painted by the San people out of shamanistic trance in an age light years removed from our own, yet expressing a desire to be in deep soul-connection with the mystery that sustains all creation.

The second was not so much a cave as a limestone quarry, and it was on Robben Island, the former prison camp off the coast of Cape Town, where Nelson Mandela spent eighteen harsh years in appalling conditions. Yet this would become a crucible of transformation for him, from violent protester to the architect of peaceful reconciliation. Here in this quarry men were driven relentlessly, hewing stone that was neither needed nor used, the work merely being imposed as a punishment. Yet it was here that the prisoners began their great enterprise of self-education. Those with academic training and gifts taught the others, including some of their captors, making this quarry the first black university in South Africa. And it was from here that the warning went out from the wiser minds among them that revenge would do nothing for the cause of freedom.

Two sacred "caves", each still redolent with the spirit that inspired them, a spirit that can continue to inspire us.

As with so many of our "landscapes", caves have many faces. They can be places that shelter us, and also places that challenge us and call us to go beyond our present limits. They can be places where we hide from what assails us, and also places to which we can withdraw to gather strength and new resolve. They can be places where we are deafened by the tumult of the storms around us, or silenced into that quietness of heart where we can truly hear the "still small voice of calm". They can be places where we feel we may starve to death, and places where we discover unexpected nourishment. They are places where we grieve for all we have loved and lost, and places where healing can begin. The cave invites us into our own innermost being. It's a risky and arduous journey, and one that may daunt us with its loneliness and gaunt dark spaces. But the pearl at the heart of the cave's oyster is that we discover, if we truly journey to the core of our being, that this is precisely where we encounter the living God.

A familiar ancient story reveals how this encounter might unfold…

THE STILL, SMALL VOICE

There was every reason to run. The fugitive had fallen foul of his enemies, and, as he saw it, God's enemies, and retribution was inevitable. He fled into the desert, frankly wishing that God would take his life. Eventually he fell into an exhausted sleep. From somewhere deep below consciousness, sustaining life touched him as he slept, and he awoke to find morsels of food and a jar of water to hand – just enough, no more, to keep him going. And so, obedient to the thrust of life within him, he journeyed on until he reached a cave where he could safely spend the night. And it was there,

in the cave, that the transforming encounter happened. "What are you doing here?" asked the voice of God. "Come out and stand in my presence on the bare mountain." The frightened fugitive did as he was told, longing for, yet dreading, the encounter with God. There came a mighty wind, but God's voice was not in its force and its clamour. Then a mighty earthquake shook the ground but God's voice was not in the volatile earth. And then came a blazing fire, but God's voice was not in its searing heat and overwhelming energy. Spent with the passion and the terror of the night, the fugitive covered his face and knelt at the mouth of the cave. And it was there, when the tumult had finally subsided, that he heard a still, small voice – just a whisper on the breath of the night air: "What are you doing here? Trust me, and do as I show you."

(Adapted from 1 Kings 19:1–18)

TIME FOR GRIEVING

Perhaps one or other of these "caves" speaks to the inner space in which you find yourself right now? Perhaps you feel the urge to hide yourself away and hope that the storm will pass you by? Perhaps you long to go deeper into the hidden recesses of your own soul, in search of the encounter with God? Perhaps you sit in the cave of your heart and weep for lost love, lost causes, broken dreams?

- Can you hear the quiet, insistent question: "What are you doing here?" How would you want to respond?

- What sustains you in your cave? Has anyone offered you that saving morsel of food and jar of water? Is there someone you know, a neighbour perhaps or a friend, or even an enemy, who desperately needs sustenance from *you*?

- The cave in South Africa was alive with the spirit of those who had gone before. What is there in your story, or in the whole human story, that inspires you to keep going, and connects

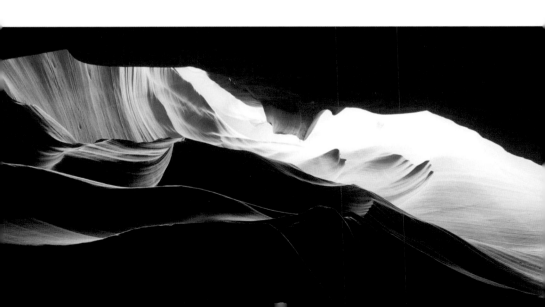

you to the long line of pilgrims who have found their own ways of expressing the perennial search for meaning in the mystery?

- The quarry on Robben Island was a place of extreme hardship that became a place of growth and transformation. Could your heart's cave be a place that is inviting you to grow?

- The "still, small voice" can only be heard in silence. How much silence and stillness is there in your life? If you feel the need to do so, how could you make space for more?

A cave is a place of burial. Bring to it all that you grieve over. Anoint those losses with your tears and leave them there. Be in that place for as long as you need to be there, and then let life itself draw you onwards, beyond your endings to your new beginnings.

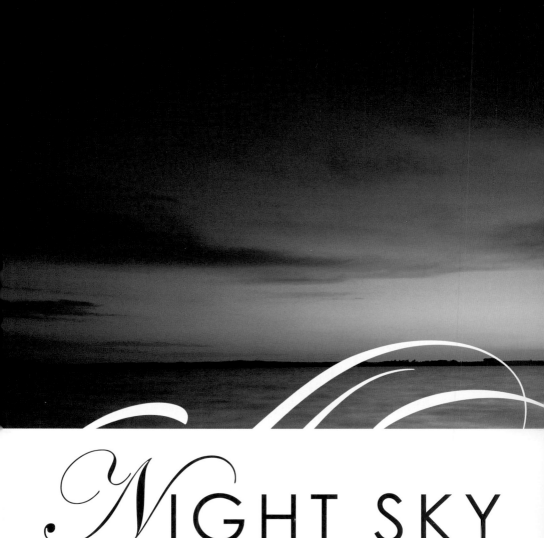

NIGHT SKY

"*Such is the time to ponder the mysteries of one's existence.*"

Brian Swimme, *The Hidden Heart of the Cosmos*

I first met God under a night sky. It was a moment I will never forget, even though I was only seven years old at the time. I was walking home from a Brownie meeting at the local church in my native Yorkshire. I reached a crossroads, where a side street joined the main road through the city. It was a dark winter evening. To my right was a public phone booth, to my left a shop that sold sweets and chocolate, well known to me by day, now closed for the night. It was just an ordinary evening, but it became, for me, an unforgettable night. I happened to look up, and above me the night sky was spread, the stars so brilliant and so close that I felt I could have stretched out my hand and plucked them down like silver apples in a celestial orchard. I could not, at that age, have articulated how I felt, and yet the feelings of that moment – more than feelings, more like *knowledge* – have never left me, but have grown clearer with every passing year. "You are utterly alone in this vast universe," the stirrings in my soul told me,

"and yet you also completely belong here." Far from being frightening, this encounter with the beyond left me feeling deeply at peace and joy-filled, and I can return to this sense of peace at any time, nearly sixty years later, simply by remembering that moment.

It is a rare human soul who is not stirred by the sight of the night sky. Astronomers estimate that there are about 100 billion stars in our own galaxy, and the Hubble telescope has provided evidence for at least 125 billion galaxies in the known universe. These numbers confound all our senses, and overload our minds' circuitry. When we reflect on our faith in God in this vast context, then there is no way we can confine God to our tiny man-made boxes of understanding. But God is inviting us not to be overwhelmed by all this wonder, but to allow it to draw our gaze far beyond ourselves and our passing pleasures and irritations, towards a reality infinitely greater than anything we can imagine, yet a reality that is, our experience reminds us, intimately engaged with every moment of our own lives. Beneath the night sky the infinite and the intimate meet and embrace right there in our own hearts.

Take some time to stand and gaze at the night sky and let it speak its truth to your being.

Let it tell you that you yourself are made of stardust, that the elements that make up your physical being were present when the first-generation stars exploded in supernova brilliance to scatter their dust across the

universe. Every particle of creation and of you yourself bears the imprinted memory of those primeval beginnings. You were being dreamed into being billions of years ago, long before Planet Earth took shape.

Let the moon show you how its silver glory is just the light reflected from a sun you cannot see, and remind you that you too emit no light of your own, but are called to reflect, as truly and clearly as you can, the light of the one in whom you have your being. Let the moonlight guard us from the illusion that we are suns, lest we stray from our destiny to be planets, orbiting in balance around the God who is our centre.

Let the shooting stars delight you, and assure you that in your life's journey there will also be blazes of light that suddenly appear out of the darkness, enlighten the dark path for a while, and lead you a little closer to your destiny. Take time to remember how those shooting stars have lit up your life in the past, and to trust that they will do so again.

As you gaze beyond the constellations, into the deep dark, reflect on the fact that on a clear day you can see, perhaps, for between twenty and sixty miles, depending on how high your vantage point, but on a dark night you can see stars that are thousands of light years distant from us. Perhaps the dark brings greater vision than the light.

And yet even the stars are not eternal. They too will come to the end of their embodied existence and return to the pure energy from which they first condensed into solid form. Not eternal, but perhaps the most potent and beautiful pointers to eternity that we could wish for. Let us join another long-distance gazer, as he reflects upon the scale of eternity and the wonder of his being, which has its own origins in that eternity…

WHEN NIGHT IS AS BRIGHT AS DAY

O God, you know every cell in my being, every movement I make, every thought that my mind shapes, every aspect of who I am and how I am. Before I utter a word, you know it already, and your hand rests upon my every breath. Such knowledge amazes me, probing depths I dare not contemplate, soaring to heights I can never hope to reach. Where would I go to flee from your gaze? Is there anywhere that your presence does not suffuse? If I fly to the skies you are there. If I sink to the depths of despair you are there. If I speed off on the wings of the dawn and find a resting place beyond the horizon, even there your hand would guide me and your arm hold me firm. I beg the darkness to envelop me and the night to wrap itself around me, but even darkness is not dark to you, and with you night is as bright as day. You created my innermost self, weaving me into being in my mother's womb, already aware of every secret that my life would hold. Lord, it is impossible to fathom your thoughts. They are as many as the grains of sand upon the shore, and even if I could ever finish counting them, there I would be, still held within your heart.

(Adapted from Psalm 139)

TIME FOR GAZING

When you find yourself standing beneath the night sky, either outwardly or inwardly, your prayer might raise questions and reflections such as these:

- God is immeasurably beyond our furthest gaze and yet closer than our own next breath. Where do you find both the infinity and the intimacy of God in your own experience?

- God has been dreaming you into existence since the universe began. The story of life from its very beginnings is imprinted on every particle of your being. What helps you to get in touch with your own deep "belonging" to creation, and the creator?

- In times of inner darkness sometimes our hearts are opened up to more profound truth than in the brighter periods of our lives. Have you ever found this to be true for you?

- In what ways have you ever tried to flee from God? Did you succeed?

- Is there time, and space, in your life simply to stand and gaze?

When all your prayers are prayed, stand beneath the stars and give your soul permission to travel beyond all words, into the living, loving heart of silence.

"The ancient astronomers, the first cosmologists, and the shamanic storytellers often told their stories at night. The concerns of the day, however important they might seem in the sunlight, usually amount to nothing more than unwelcome distractions in the night when the great story is told in the glow from the fire's embers and Moon's journey through the branched shadows of the trees. It is in the peace that the night brings that something immense can stir in the depths of the listener. Late, very late, after the sun is gone — such is the time for the great surprises deep in the listener's soul. Such is the time to ponder the mysteries of one's existence."

(Brian Swimme, *The Hidden Heart of the Cosmos*)

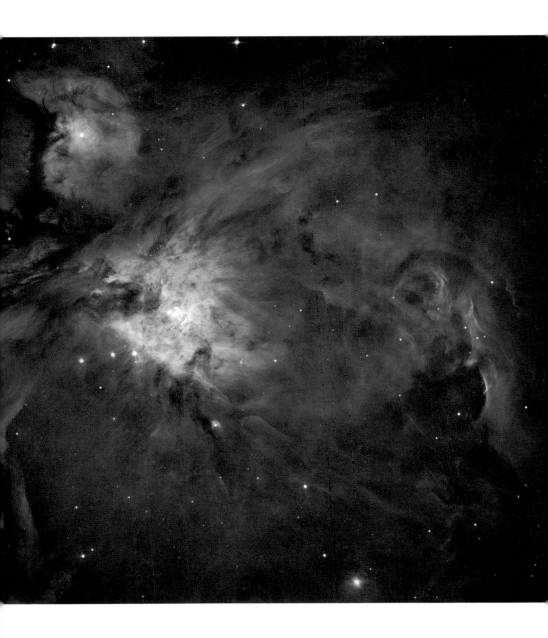

ACKNOWLEDGMENTS

Corbis: p. 2 Micha Pawlitzki; p. 6 Barrett & MacKay/All Canada Photos; p. 9 Harpur Garden Library; p. 12 Destinations; p. 14 David Nunuk/First Light; p. 16 Paul Freytag; p. 20 Blaine Harrington III; p. 32 Jim Craigmyle; pp. 34–35 James Randklev; p. 36 Gavin Hellier/JAI; p. 53 Momatiuk – Eastcott; p. 59 Radius Images; p. 64 Fotofeeling/Westend61; p. 66 John Lund; pp. 67, 71 Martin Harvey; p. 70 O. Alamany & E. Vicens; p. 80 Nick Rains; p. 88 Rolf Hicker/All Canada Photos; p. 91 STScI/NASA

iStock: pp. 1, 44, 82, 84 AVTG; p. 4 kavram; p. 8 Dina Magnat; p. 10 Pauline S Mills; p. 11 Arie J. Jager; p. 13t Amy Riley; p. 13b Susan Fox; p. 19 ranplett; p. 22 Sara Winter; p. 25 antony spencer; p. 26 Ingo Meckmann; p. 28 Carlos Caetano; pp. 29t, 37, 72 Ken Canning; p. 29b OGphoto; pp. 30–31 Andrew Clelland; p. 38 DeborahMaxemow; p. 39 William Walsh; p. 40 Denis Jr. Tangney; p. 42 Peter Mukherjee; pp. 43, 58l Nikada; p. 47 Björn Kindler; p. 48 Dean Turner; p. 50l ingmar wesemann; p. 50r saluha; p. 52 David Evans; pp. 54, 56b, 60, 62–63 Sze Fei Wong; p. 56t David Ciemny; p. 57 Mayumi Terao; p. 58m Daniel Ross; p. 58r Ola Dusegård; p. 69 jin bai; p. 74 Tupungato; p. 76 hougaard malan; p. 77 Ruvan Boshoff; p. 78 Milen Slavov; p. 79 Mableen; p. 81 Jeff Hathaway; pp. 85–86 Evgeny Kuklev; p. 89 Alexandr Smushko; p. 93 Dimitar Marinov

A Lion Book
an imprint of
Lion Hudson plc
Wilkinson House, Jordan Hill Road,
Oxford OX2 8DR, England
www.lionhudson.com
ISBN 978 0 7459 5528 5

Distributed by:
UK: Marston Book Services, PO Box 269, Abingdon, Oxon, OX14 4YN
USA: Trafalgar Square Publishing, 814 N. Franklin Street, Chicago, IL 60610
USA Christian Market: Kregel Publications, PO Box 2607, Grand Rapids,
Michigan 49501

First edition 2011
10 9 8 7 6 5 4 3 2 1

A catalogue record for this book is available from the British Library

Typeset in 11/14 Adobe Garamond Pro
Printed and bound in China